PRAISE FOR LOW CARBON DIET

"The book is fabulous! It couldn't be more timely. It's practical, accessible and effective. Getting people to take on Global Warming at a personal level is critical to tackling the issue. The *Low Carbon Diet* can make a huge difference."
Denis Hayes, Co-founder, Earth Day

"David Gershon has created a step-by-step program, à la Weight Watchers, designed to reduce a person's carbon footprint. . . . Replete with checklists and illustrations, this user-friendly guide is a serious attempt at changing American energy-consumption behavior. . . . The timing for a book offering day-to-day solutions to an overwhelming global problem couldn't be better."
The Christian Science Monitor

"*Low Carbon Diet* couldn't be timelier in providing people an action plan for addressing climate change, just when the collective consciousness seems to be bending in that direction. . . . The book helps self-organized teams take action to dramatically reduce their carbon footprint."
Leverage Points, Pegasus Communications

"A 'how-to' guide for people to change their energy habits. David Gershon has succeeded in making carbon-dieting sound like a win-win proposition: save energy, save money and, most importantly, save the planet."
Eileen Claussen, President of the Pew Center on Global Climate Change

"Just as the consciousness-raising groups of the women's movement changed America overnight at no cost to anyone, so can the *Low Carbon Diet* inspire environmental consciousness-raising groups. Their results can restore the Earth rather than destroy it....and at virtually no cost."
Susan Davis, President, CapitalMissions.com

"FINALLY. . . . there's the *Low Carbon Diet*. The program is intelligently and imaginatively built to be user-friendly, easy and fun!! I made new friends, was encouraged that others feel as passionately about safeguarding our planet as I do, and was supported by my LCD Team in taking really significant actions! Amazing!! Now I'm working with new and old friends to bring the LCD program to my community, and finally feeling a sense of hope for our future and the future of our Earth."
Patty Goodwin, Low Carbon Diet participant

"The *Low Carbon Diet* is amazingly effective at promoting true, sustainable change. The realities of our very green family's carbon consumption were sobering, but David Gershon's program has given us an easy-to-implement plan for dramatically lowering it."
Nan and Andy Satter, Low Carbon Diet participants

PRAISE FOR THE
GREEN LIVING HANDBOOK
(on which *Low Carbon Diet* is based)

"This program is the first step-by-step plan for turning environmental concern into action."
The Chicago Tribune

"A movement . . . of unquestionable zeal is challenging consumption at the grass roots . . . local support groups called EcoTeams are methodically helping members reduce the amount and kind of material that flows in and out of homes."
The New York Times

"The program offers a common-sense approach to environmentalism. One participant says, 'I love our neighborhood and this is an opportunity for us to make it an even nicer place to live together'."
The Boston Globe

"The biggest thing about the *Green Living Handbook* is that it is helping people change behavior. You could do information campaigns and hope people change, but as a city, this is a better investment."
The Kansas City Star

"EcoTeams help people build community while working toward something they believe in. It takes a village to save the Earth."
Family Circle

"The *Green Living* program is skillfully designed to be attractive to individuals, local governments, and businesses . . . It has demonstrated results . . . it can make a real difference. In our work with communities across America, this is exactly the sort of tool for which they are searching."
Molly Olson, Executive Director, President's Council on Sustainable Development (Clinton Administration)

"The *Green Living* program opens up a new category of policy instruments having to do with voluntary change. The program is more sophisticated than information campaigns, since it gives people the personal support they need to change their ingrained habits of how they use resources."
Paul de Jongh, Deputy Director General for Environmental Protection, The Netherlands, Author, Dutch "Green Plan"

"One of the most enlightening and useful programs that I have had the privilege to encounter . . . It provides a starting point for America's citizens and communities to begin the journey of becoming more sustainable."
Michele Perrault, Past President, The Sierra Club

Low Carbon Diet ℠

A 30 Day Program to Lose 5,000 Pounds

David Gershon

Low Carbon Diet
ISBN 13: 978-0-9630327-2-0
ISBN 10: 0-9630327-2-0
Copyright © 2006 David Gershon
Printed in Canada

9 8 7 6 5 4

Published by:
Empowerment Institute
P.O. Box 428
Woodstock, New York 12498
info@empowermentinstitute.net
www.empowermentinstitute.net

This book is printed on 100% post consumer waste
Forest Stewardship Certified recycled paper, using plant-based inks.
The paper is processed chlorine free and manufactured using biogas energy.

By using 100% post consumer waste recycled paper instead of virgin fibers,
this edition saved:

Trees: 38
Solid waste: 2,415lb
Water: 22,793gal
Suspended particles in the water: 15.3lb
Air emissions: 5,303lb
Natural gas: 5,526ft^3

DEDICATION

Low Carbon Diet is dedicated to our planet's future generations.

ACKNOWLEDGEMENTS

Many people have contributed to the development of this program. I wish to thank my esteemed colleague Eve Baer for her research on some of the actions, program design, editing, beautiful photographs, and collaboration over the years; Dan Wetzel for his charming illustrations; Llyn Peabody for helping implement a successful pilot version of this program; Michael Armstrong and Carol Ann Kampuries for their research in assigning CO_2 reduction values to the actions; Susan Anderson for her inspiration and encouragement to test these ideas in the City of Portland, Oregon; Andrea Stern for her contribution to the EcoTeam program from which a number of the actions in this book were derived; Craig Hamilton for his editing and support; Steve Busch for his elegant graphic design of this book; the residents of Portland, Oregon, who participated in the pilot and demonstrated the readiness of our culture for a program like this; and the many thousands of people around the world who participated in EcoTeams and proved that given the right tools, people can and will adopt environmentally sustainable lifestyle practices. Lastly, I wish to thank my wife, Gail Straub, for her loving partnership and support of me over the years in doing this work.

TABLE OF CONTENTS

SECTION THREE – EMPOWERING OTHERS TO LOSE UNWANTED POUNDS

SECTION FOUR – CO_2 REDUCTION ACTION PLAN

SECTION FIVE – PROGRAM SUPPORT TOOLS

INTRODUCTION

Global warming is changing our world. Severe hurricanes, tornadoes, heat waves, and flooding are becoming commonplace. The consequences, including loss of life, economic disruption, and population dislocation are growing each year. As individuals living on the planet at this moment in time, we face a challenge no generation has ever had to face. We need to dramatically change the manner in which we use the Earth's natural resources. And we need to do this soon or we will significantly increase the severity of climate-induced natural disasters.

The primary cause of global warming is carbon dioxide emitted into the atmosphere through the burning of fossil fuels—gasoline, coal, oil, and natural gas—which we use to power our cars and homes and to produce the goods we consume. The typical American household generates 55,000 pounds of carbon dioxide annually. Taken collectively, US households directly produce about 8% of the planet's carbon dioxide emissions, and through our purchases we are indirectly responsible for another 17%. By contrast, the typical German household contributes 27,000 pounds and the average Swedish household's contribution is only 15,000 pounds. Clearly, we have much room for improvement.

If the bad news is that individual Americans are a major part of the problem, the good news is that we can also be a major part of the solution. By making specific, targeted changes to actions we already take every day, we can significantly reduce our CO_2 emissions.

If you're among those who understand the seriousness of our plight, you probably feel called to do something about it. And like a lot of us, you're now asking: Where do I begin? Which are the important actions to take? How do I take them? And if I do take them, will it really make a difference given the magnitude of the problem?

This book answers those questions. It will show you how, in just a single month, you can make enough simple adjustments to your lifestyle to reduce your annual CO_2 output by at least 5,000 pounds. And how, if you're interested, you can even reduce your CO_2 footprint to zero.

The program described in this book is based on a tried and true methodology grounded in extensive research. Over the past two decades, I have developed environmental behavior change programs that have helped several hundred thousand people demonstrably lessen their toll on the planet. American households using this simple methodology have reduced their environmental footprint by over 25% *and* sustained these changes over time.

Participants in these programs represent a cross-section of political and religious ideologies. They range from people who view themselves as environmentalists to those who just think it makes good sense to use resources more efficiently. What they all have in common is that they need help translating their good intentions into action.

An encouraging pattern emerged when I began working with social networks, faith communities, neighborhoods, civic groups, and workplaces. I observed that once the initial group of people took up the program, it would often achieve a tipping point and, through word-of-mouth, rapidly spread throughout that community. It often reached as many as 85% of the people in a particular sub-culture. Because most people want to do the right thing for the environment, there was no inherent resistance to participation. Once I discovered this desire among participants to share the program with others, I furthered the process along by providing simple tools for spreading it.

I believe that the issue of global warming is extraordinarily primed for this type of grassroots empowerment process. The daily effects of climate change combined with the continually rising costs of energy have gotten everyone's attention. People want to move out of helplessness and fear. They want to take matters into their own hands and become part of the solution.

When I asked participants in my environmental programs why they took time out of their busy lives to make these changes, the most common response was "to create a better future for my children and future generations." This aspiration is even more relevant for the issue of global warming.

If we ordinary Americans reduce our carbon dioxide footprint, we can have a disproportionate influence in turning the tide on global warming. When we, the consumers and voters, become part of the global warming solution, businesses and politicians will not be far behind. As the saying goes, when the people lead, the leaders will follow. And as America—the planet's greatest contributor to climate change—takes responsibility for reducing its carbon footprint, the impact will inevitably ripple out.

An extraordinary moment for change has arrived. Feedback from the Earth is telling us it is time to act. Al Gore's profound movie "An Inconvenient Truth" has created a groundswell of interest among ordinary citizens who want to do their part. The stars are in perfect alignment for change. This is a heroic time calling for heroic action.

You can lead the way and this book will show you how. It builds on my two decades of learning and a highly successful pilot of this program where participants achieved a 22% (6,700 pound) annual CO_2 reduction. The actions in this book are easy to take and are accompanied by lighthearted illustrations that make it fun. Each has a CO_2 reduction value so you can set and achieve your reduction goal. The program can be done as an individual household or as a small group of friends, neighbors, or co-workers—what I call an EcoTeam. Experience has shown that doing it as a team can provide extra motivation to follow through. But either approach works.

The program is divided into three sections. First, you work on adopting climate-friendly lifestyle practices. You learn how to change habit patterns established over the course of your life that you rarely think about but that are easy to change once you know how to do it. Then you move to your household systems. These are the mechanical parts of your life. Taking action here will have a long-term impact and will not require much thinking about it again. Once you have reduced your own CO_2 footprint, the last section shows you how to help others do the same. You learn how to invite people in your social network, workplace, community, or children's school to become part of the global warming solution.

I am in awe of the potential for this moment to be truly catalytic. I know we can make the needed changes happen, and I am hopeful this book can play a significant role. I wish you well in this journey and thank you for doing your part. Godspeed . . .

HOW THE PROGRAM WORKS

1. Select from the menu of actions in this workbook those that help you reduce your carbon dioxide (CO_2) emissions by a minimum of 5,000 pounds.

2. You can do the program either with your household family members or as part of a peer support group of friends, neighbors, co-workers, or members of your faith community or civic organization—an EcoTeam. A good size for an EcoTeam is 5 to 8 households.

3. In either format, the program is designed to be completed in 4 meetings that take place every 10 to 14 days. A team initiator runs the meetings using scripts located in the support section of this workbook. Meetings last 1.5 to 2 hours, with several hours needed between meetings to take the actions selected. If you do the program as an individual household and live with others, turn your household members into a team and adapt the meeting scripts accordingly. If you live alone and choose to do this on your own, use the program's suggested time sequence as a structure to keep you motivated.

4. In the team program, the first meeting—the Team Building Meeting—is used to create your support system, learn how to calculate your CO_2 footprint, (www.empowermentinstitute.net/lcd) and create an action plan to reduce it (pages 51–54). During meetings 2 to 4, team participants report on actions taken and describe their action plans for the next section. The team provides support and inspiration for everyone to carry out their plans.

5. Each program action in this workbook indicates the pounds of CO_2 your household can save. Whatever your emissions are at the start of the program, you are encouraged to select actions to help you achieve a 5,000 pound reduction or greater. If you have already taken many CO_2 reduction actions, you will start at a higher level of achievement. The typical American household is Level 4.

	Annual Household CO2 Emissions (pounds)
Level 1	80,000 and above
Level 2	70,000 - 79,999
Level 3	60,000 - 69,999
Level 4	50,000 - 59,999
Level 5	40,000 - 49,999
Level 6	30,000 - 39,999
Level 7	20,000 - 29,999
Level 8	10,000 - 19,999
Level 9	1,000 – 9,999
Level 10	Carbon Neutral (less than 1000)

That's it! Enjoy making your contribution to the quality of life of future generations.

SECTION ONE:
COOL LIFESTYLE PRACTICES

1. Dumping On Garbage
Reducing Solid Waste

WHY ACT?

The average US household produces about 4.5 pounds of solid waste per day. About a third of it is packaging used only to get the item to your home. Producing this waste requires energy for extraction of the raw materials, manufacturing them into various goods, and transportation throughout the whole process. Every pound of solid waste that goes to the landfill generates 2 pounds of greenhouse gases. These come from transporting and land-filling the waste and from the natural decomposition that occurs in an anaerobic environment. This action will help you reduce the solid waste you send to the landfill.

CO₂ REDUCTION ACTION

❍ If you are recycling less than you could or not recycling at all, get sorting guidelines from your local recycling center or trash collection service. Set up bags, boxes, or bins (your household recycling center) according to these guidelines.

❍ To reduce packaging, bring your own cloth bags when shopping, buy in bulk, purchase items with the least packaging, and buy reusable items.

❍ To reduce junk mail, write to: DirectMail.com, National Do Not Mail Registry, Prince Frederick, MD, 20678. Request that they remove your name from all 3rd class mailing lists. You can make your request at no charge via the internet at www.DirectMail.com/Junk_Mail.

❍ Contact those companies still sending you junk mail and request to be removed from their lists. You can use their self-addressed return envelope, fax or call the 800 number for customer service.

TIME & MATERIALS

❍ 30 to 60 minutes to get guidelines and expand or set-up your recycling system; a few minutes a day communicating to companies that continue sending you junk mail.

❍ Bags or boxes, markers, cloth bags, pen, paper, envelopes, stamps.

GOAL

Reduce the amount of your weekly waste by one garbage can size.

CO₂ CREDIT

Note: Check the box as you take each action.

❏ For setting up a system to make sure that *all* your recyclable waste gets recycled, credit yourself with 1,300 pounds.

❏ If you reduce the amount of waste produced by your household by one level or more, credit yourself according to the table below.

Amount of weekly waste before taking action	Amount of weekly waste after taking action	Credit yourself with the following CO_2 reduction
90 gallon trash container or equivalent	60 gallon trash container or equivalent	3,120 lbs
60 gallon trash container or equivalent	35 gallon trash container or equivalent	2,600 lbs
35 gallon trash container or equivalent	20 gallon trash container or equivalent	1,560 lbs

Note: If you reduce your waste by more than one level, add the reductions together.

By doing this action I lost _____ pounds!

8

2. AM I CLEAN YET?

Reducing Hot Water Used in Showers

WHY ACT?

How much water do you need to get your body clean? Many people spend 10 minutes or more in the shower. Heating hot water for a 10-minute shower can generate as much as 4 pounds of CO_2. By staying in the shower for 5 minutes instead of 10 and ensuring that you have a low-flow showerhead, you can have a pleasurable shower and annually save several hundred pounds of CO_2. A bath can use up to twice the amount of hot water you need for a 5-minute shower. Use an efficient shower to get clean, and use a bath or occasional long shower for relaxation.

CO₂ REDUCTION ACTION

○ If you don't already have low-flow showerheads on your showers, purchase and install them.

○ Time your average shower.

○ Reduce this time so you are consistently at 5 minutes or under.

TIME AND MATERIALS

○ 30 to 60 minutes to purchase a low-flow shower head from a local hardware store or green catalog, a few minutes to install it. You actually increase your free time by taking planet-friendly showers.

○ Low-flow shower head, adjustable wrench, a watch or clock.

GOAL

A 5-minute shower with a low-flow showerhead.

CO₂ CREDIT

Note: Check the box as you take each action.

❑ For each person in your household who reduces their shower time to 5 minutes or less, credit 300 pounds of CO_2 reduction per person per year.

❑ Install a low-flow showerhead and reduce annual CO_2 emissions by 250 pounds (for each one you install).

3. SCRUB-A-DUB TUB

Reducing Water Used for Washing Dishes

WHY ACT?

Each time you run your dishwasher, you produce approximately 2 pounds of CO_2. Hand-washing dishes inefficiently can use up to 15 gallons of hot water or almost 3 pounds of CO_2 per dishwashing. Through greater dishwashing efficiency you can reduce your CO_2 footprint in this area by 25% or more.

CO_2 REDUCTION ACTION

○ Dishwasher: Run only when you have a full load. Scrape off food, but don't rinse dishes before loading. Use the energy-saving setting to dry dishes ("air dry" rather than "heat dry").

○ Hand-washing: Wash dishes in a tub of hot soapy water. Fill a second tub for rinsing dishes.

○ Make sure your kitchen faucet has an aerator. Aerators reduce water flow by about 25% and produce a water stream that is every bit as good for washing dishes, hands, or fruits and vegetables.

Note: When it's time to replace your dishwasher, buy Energy Star®. Information about Energy Star® dishwashers can be found at www.energystar.gov

TIME & MATERIALS

○ You will save time through greater efficiency in your dishwashing.

○ Sink, tub, dishwasher, biodegradable dishwashing soap.

GOAL

If you use a dishwasher, reduce dishwasher use by one load per week, and avoid using the "heat dry" setting to dry your dishes. For hand-washing, always wash dishes in one basin and rinse in a second basin.

CO_2 CREDIT

Note: Check the box as you take each action.

❑ For reducing dishwasher use by one load per week, credit yourself 100 pounds of avoided CO_2 per year.

❑ For minimizing hot water use in hand dishwashing, credit yourself with 125 pounds of avoided CO_2 emissions annually.

❑ Bonus: If you have an Energy Star® dishwasher or plan to buy one within a year, credit yourself an additional 125 pounds of annual CO_2 savings.

4. Wear It Again Sam

Washing and Drying Clothes Efficiently

WHY ACT?

Typical electric clothes washers and dryers generate 5 pounds of CO_2 per washer/dryer cycle. Do your clothes really need to be washed after one wearing, or will the simple touch of an iron or the removal of a dirty spot allow you to wear them again?

For laundry machine-washed in hot water, 90% of the energy goes to heat the water, while only 10% powers the machine itself. In most cases, washing clothes in cold water gets them just as clean as washing them in warm or hot water, and the CO_2 savings are substantial—about 2 pounds per load.

The new, front-loading washing machines save even more energy by reducing the amount of water—hot or cold—used in each load by about 50%. These washers also have a faster spin cycle than conventional machines, so they remove more of the water from your clothes, reducing the energy it takes to dry them.

CO_2 REDUCTION ACTION

❍ Wear clothes until they are actually dirty. Hang them up after each wearing to let them air out naturally.

❍ Use an iron to touch up creases or a wet cloth and a little soap to get a spot out when the rest of the garment is clean.

❍ When you wash your clothes, be energy-efficient by doing full loads and using cold water for washing and rinsing.

❍ Dry full loads or use a clothesline instead.

❍ Separate loads for fast- and slow-drying clothes and use moisture or automatic settings rather than the timer.

TIME & MATERIALS

❍ A few minutes to iron, remove a spot, or hang clothes up to dry.

❍ An iron, wet cloth, soap, clothesline, drying rack, washer, and dryer.

GOAL

Reduce the number of loads you wash in warm or hot water by washing and rinsing in cold water whenever possible. Reduce the number of dryer loads by at least one per week by reducing washing needs and drying clothes on a clothesline when possible.

CO_2 CREDIT

Note: Check the box as you take each action.

❏ If you switch one load of laundry each week from hot to cold water, credit yourself 100 pounds of CO_2 annually.

❏ For eliminating the need for one dryer load each week, credit yourself 260 pounds of CO_2 each year.

❏ Bonus: If you plan to buy an Energy Star® front-loading washer in the next year, credit yourself 500 pounds of annual CO_2 savings.

5. BETTER A SWEATER

Turning Down the Heating Thermostat

WHY ACT?

During cold weather, many people set their thermostat a little warmer than necessary. Home heating accounts for over a quarter of your energy bill. People who live in colder climates and heat their homes typically generate 8,800 pounds of CO_2 emissions annually. You can turn down your thermostat and still be quite comfortable. This action will show you how.

CO_2 REDUCTION ACTION

○ During the day when people are home, set your thermostat at "sweater" temperature: between 65°–68°F.

○ Before going to bed at night or when everyone is out of the house set the thermostat to "blanket" temperature: between 55°–58°F.

○ Consider installing a programmable thermostat so you make sure the heat is always at the temperature you wish. This can reduce your heating bill by up to 20%.

TIME & MATERIALS

○ A few seconds to set the thermostat. A few hours to purchase and install a programmable thermostat.

○ A programmable thermostat.

GOAL

Set your thermostat at 65°–68°F during the day and 55°–58°F at night.

CO_2 CREDIT

Note: Check the box as you take the action.

❑ Changing your thermostat habits and setting your thermostat to 65°–68°F when someone is active in the house and 55°–58°F at night leads to an annual CO_2 reduction of 1,400 pounds.

6. Plug Your Electricity Leaks

Turning Appliances All the Way Off

WHY ACT?

America's TVs consume the output of 21 large power plants. It takes one large power plant to supply power for all these TV sets shut-off! Many other types of home appliances use electricity even when turned off. In an average home, the common mix of televisions, DVD and video recorders, CD players and other appliances use about 50 watts of electricity 24 hours per day. Over a year, that produces over 600 lbs of CO_2.

CO_2 REDUCTION ACTION

❍ Identify the appliances that leak the most electricity such as televisions and DVD recorders and plug them into a switched cord or power strip.

❍ Turn off the power to these appliances when not in use.

❍ If possible, unplug any devices and chargers that have a block-shaped transformer on the plug when they are not in use (or turn off with a power strip).

❍ When you buy new equipment, look for the Energy Star® label. Appliances that meet new Energy Star® guidelines use much less standby power.

TIME & MATERIALS

❍ Extension cord or power strip with an on-off switch. A few seconds every day to flip the switch.

GOAL

Home appliance energy leaks plugged.

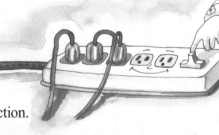

CO_2 CREDIT

Note: Check the box as you take each action.

❑ Credit yourself with 600 lbs of CO_2 reduction for completely turning off electronic equipment when not in use.

7. CHILL-IN

Cooling Your House More Efficiently

WHY ACT?

If you use air conditioning, you may be overcooling your home or apartment beyond what you need to be comfortable. This action will help you cool your house in a way that provides comfort to you and the planet.

CO2 REDUCTION ACTION

○ When purchasing your air conditioner:
  - Buy the most efficient model; look for one with an Energy Star® rating.
  - Make sure the unit is the correct size for the amount of space you are cooling and, if possible, install the unit in the shade to reduce its workload.

○ When installing your air conditioner:
  - If your air conditioner must be in the sun, build a protective shade or screen over it. Make sure this does not block air circulation. This increases the unit's efficiency by 5–10%.

○ To maintain your air conditioner:
  - Inspect the filter every month during cooling seasons. Clean and replace the filter as needed. A clogged filter can use 5% more energy than a clean one. Clean the entire unit at least once a year, according to the manufacturer's instructions.
  - If you have a central air-conditioning system, have it tuned up and the coils cleaned every three years. Regular servicing of a central air system can yield a 10–20% energy savings.

○ To effectively operate your air conditioner:
  - Set your thermostat at "short sleeve" temperature: 78°F. If the temperature outside is the same or cooler than that, just open the windows. If you have an older air conditioner that does not have the temperatures marked on the dial, use a room thermometer. For every degree you raise the thermostat, you save 3–5% of your cooling costs.
  - Install a timer on your room air conditioner or an Energy Star® rated programmable thermostat for your central air-conditioning system so you don't have to leave it on when it's not needed. It's a myth that it's more efficient to leave an air conditioner on than to shut it off and have to recool a home later. It pays to turn off your air conditioner when you will be gone for more than an hour.

- If you don't wish to use an air conditioner or you want to reduce the amount of energy your air conditioner uses, consider keeping your shades or curtains drawn during the heat of the day and planting trees on the western, southern, and eastern sides of your house. A home's indoor temperature can rise as much as 20°F if the windows are not shaded.

TIME & MATERIALS

❍ 5 minutes to clean your filter periodically; 5 minutes to make an appointment to have it serviced professionally; some more time to do the job yourself.

❍ Materials for protective shades, filters, vacuum cleaner, timer, or programmable thermostat.

GOAL

Place your air conditioner in the shade, clean or replace the filter, and raise your thermostat by 4 degrees or up to the next highest setting.

CO_2 CREDIT

Note: Check the box as you take each action.

❏ Replace or clean the filter as recommended for a 350 pound annual CO_2 savings.

❏ Raise your thermostat by 4 degrees or up to the next highest setting to reduce your CO_2 emissions by 20 pounds per month. If you use AC for three months a year, your savings is 60 pounds; if you use AC year-round, your savings is 240 pounds.

❏ Replace your old air conditioner with a new Energy Star® model within the next year and give yourself credit for 600 pounds CO_2 savings.

8. THINK BEFORE YOU GO

Reducing Vehicle Miles Traveled

WHY ACT?

U.S. residents drive an average of 10,000 miles per year per capita—for every adult, teenager, and toddler. For a car that gets 20 mpg, each mile driven is equivalent to a pound of CO_2, which means the emissions add up fast. Learning how to reduce the amount of vehicle miles traveled (VMT) is one of the most high-leverage actions you can take. With planning, most people can achieve reductions of 20% (1,650 pounds of annual CO_2 reduction) or more while still maintaining an active, fulfilling lifestyle. This action will show you how.

CO_2 REDUCTION ACTION

○ Start by inviting each member of your household who drives a car to join you in keeping a trip diary for a typical week. Note the destination and mileage of each trip. Divide trips into commute and non-commute. For each trip, indicate if it could combine one or more activities, such as food shopping and going to work, and if other modes of transport are available: bus, bike, walking, car/van pool.

○ At the end of the week, add up the commute and non-commute miles traveled by you and the other members of your household. Project this over a year, including any trips you normally take that didn't fall into this week period.

○ Create a plan to reduce your household's single occupancy vehicle miles traveled by 20% or more over the next year. Following are some examples of how you could achieve your goal:
  - *Commute Trips:* Telecommuting (working from a home office), carpooling, walking, or biking one or more days a week can reduce your commute VMT by 20% or more.
  - *Non-Commute Trips*: Food shopping and household errands: Making a list of all items you need, buying in larger quantities, combining with other trips on the way, and asking other household members if they need anything when you go on an errand can reduce VMT in this category by as much as 50% a week.
  - *Non Commute Trips*: Children's school and after-school activities: Carpooling with other parents could reduce this category of VMT by 20% to 80%. Organize at the destination site with other parents.

❍ If you evaluate each typical trip in this way, you will be amazed at what is possible with relatively little effort and forethought! Most of us are accustomed to driving places without thinking about it. We can get just as accustomed to thinking before we propel a several-thousand-pound car to the corner store to purchase a quart of milk.

Here's a chart to help you figure the fuel efficiency of your vehicle:

How to use this chart:
Fill your tank with gas and record your car's odometer reading in Line 2. Then, drive until the car needs refueling. Fill your tank again and record the odometer reading in Line 1, and the amount of gas it took to fill the tank in Line 4. Subtract Line 2 from Line 1 to get the total for Line 3. Divide Line 3 by Line 4 to get your average miles per gallon (line 5).

MILES PER GALLON CALCULATOR

	Vehicle 1	Vehicle 2	Vehicle 3
Line 1: Mileage 2nd time fill tank:	_____	_____	_____
Line 2: Mileage 1st time fill tank:	_____	_____	_____
Line 3: Subtract mileage: (Distance traveled)	_____	_____	_____
Line 4: Divide by gallons of gas you added:	_____	_____	_____
Line 5: Miles per gallon:	_____	_____	_____

Note: Air travel generates as much CO2 per passenger as traveling the same distance by driving yourself in a car. For every 100 miles less you travel via plane you reduce your CO2 emissions by 100 pounds. Consider this when you arrange travel for business or pleasure.

TIME AND MATERIALS

❍ A minute or so each car trip to record your mileage; 2 hours or so to create your VMT reduction plan.

❍ Your automobile, pen, paper, bike, walking or running shoes, bus pass, and creativity.

GOAL

20% reduction or more in annual vehicle miles traveled per automobile.

CO₂ CREDIT

Note: Check the box as you take each action.

❏ Calculate your current CO₂ emissions from driving by finding the number of miles you drive annually in the first column. Follow the row and column you select to find the annual CO₂ emissions for your car. Divide this number by 5 to find the CO₂ credit from reducing VMT by 20%.
CO₂ credit = _____.

For example: If you drive 10,000 miles annually and get 30 mpg, your annual CO₂ output is 6,667 pounds. Divide that by 5 to get a savings of 1,333 pounds of CO₂ (if you reduce your driving by 20%).

CO₂ Emissions from Vehicles (pounds)

Miles driven/ year	15 mpg	20 mpg	25 mpg	30 mpg	35 mpg	40 mpg	45 mpg	50 mpg	60 mpg
5,000	6,666	5,000	4,000	3,333	2,857	2,500	2,222	2,000	1,667
7,500	10,000	7,500	6,000	5,000	4,286	3,750	3,333	3,000	2,500
10,000	13,333	10,000	8,000	6,667	5,714	5,000	4,444	4,000	3,333
12,500	16,667	12,500	10,500	8,333	7,143	6,250	5,556	5,000	4,167
15,000	20,000	15,000	12,000	10,000	8,571	7,500	6,667	6,000	5,550
20,000	26,667	20,000	16,000	13,333	11,429	10,000	8,889	8,000	6,667

9. DRIVE EARTH SMART

Fuel Efficient Driving

WHY ACT?

Did you know that you can save 10–30% of your fuel costs and the CO_2 that represents by driving smart? This action will not only save you money and the planet CO_2; it will also make you a safer driver. Here's how to drive smart.

CO_2 REDUCTION ACTION

○ Before you even pull out of the driveway:
   - If your household has more than one vehicle, drive the more fuel-efficient model when you have a choice.
   - Plan your route, including commutes to work. The best route may not be the shortest, but the one that prevents idling in traffic. In city driving, up to one-third of your fuel can be wasted through idling.
   - Rid your car of any unnecessary weight. You lose 1% fuel efficiency for every extra 100 pounds.

○ When driving on the highway:
   - Maintain a steady speed, using your cruise control device if you have one. For most vehicles, 55 is the most fuel efficient highway speed and will save you up to 20–30% in fuel costs compared to driving at 75 mph. It's also safer.

○ When driving on secondary roads:
   - Anticipate stops and slowdowns, decelerating steadily to save gas.
   - When appropriate, drive between 45 and 55 mph, the most fuel efficient range.
   - Turn your engine off when you stop for a minute or two, such as at railroad crossings. It's a myth that it's more fuel-efficient to leave your engine running for a few minutes than to turn it off and restart it.

TIME AND MATERIALS

○ No time at all and a light foot on the pedal.

GOAL

Develop Earth-Smart driving practices.

CO_2 CREDIT

Note: Check the box as you take the action.

❏ For implementing these fuel efficient driving practices, credit your household for saving 55 gallons of gasoline per year, which represents 1,100 pounds of annual CO_2 reduction per auto.

10. CHEW ON THIS FOR A WHILE

Eating Lower On the Food Chain

WHY ACT?

One of the most important actions you can take to reduce your CO_2 emissions is to broaden your diet and become less dependent on meat. Livestock produced by factory and rainforest farming are inefficient at converting grains and other resources into useable food. Beef requires 16 pounds of grain just to produce a pound of meat. Add to that the resources used for producing grain, transporting meat to market, and packaging. A person with a red meat diet emits the global warming equivalent of approximately 5,000 pounds of CO_2 a year more than a person with a vegetarian diet. This action will help you reduce the meat meals you eat.

CO_2 REDUCTION ACTION

○ Review your diet. See how much meat you eat and look for opportunities to substitute vegetarian meals.

○ Look through cookbooks for tasty vegetarian recipes.

○ Gather household members and discuss this action with them, encouraging them to join you in enjoying a vegetarian meal at home.

○ Commit to eating at least one less meat meal a week.

○ If you eat meat, consider choosing "free range" or "organic" varieties that will contribute to a healthy environment and greater health for you and your family.

Note: If you want to take this action a step further, purchase local produce and dairy products or participate in community-supported agriculture. You might also wish to grow your own food. Buying local or growing your own food can reduce the energy needed to transport produce by 1,000 miles or more.

TIME & MATERIALS

○ Vegetables, grains, fruits, and nuts; a vegetarian cookbook or two.

GOAL

To switch from meat to vegetarian meals one or more days a week.

CO₂ CREDIT

Note: Check the box as you take each action.

❑ For each day of the week your household ongoingly switches from meat-based to vegetarian meals, credit 700 pounds of CO_2 reduction per year.

NOTES

_____

_____

_____

_____

_____

_____

_____

_____

_____

_____

_____

_____

_____

Section Two:
Cool Household Systems

11. Meet Your Water Heater
Making Your Water Heater Efficient

WHY ACT?

You probably don't think about your water heater unless your shower turns cold. Your water heater, however, represents about 20% of the CO_2 emissions of your home. If your heater was designed before 1989, there is much room for improving its efficiency. This action will help you heat your water and not the surrounding air.

CO_2 REDUCTION ACTION

○ For maximum water heater efficiency:
- Set your water heater thermostat to 120°F.
- Make an appointment for a water heater tune-up.
- Put water setting to "off" or "pilot" when you go on a trip.

○ To insulate your water heating system:
- If your water heater was manufactured before 1989, install an insulating blanket.
- Insulate the first 5 feet of hot water pipes with foam sleeves (but make sure the foam does not touch the exhaust on gas water heaters).

○ If you want to eliminate almost all emissions from water heating, research whether your home is well suited to a solar hot water heating system. Visit www.eere.energy.gov/solar

Note: Do not install insulating blankets on gas water heaters!

TIME & MATERIALS

○ 30 minutes to several hours depending on what has to be done.

○ An insulating blanket and foam sleeves.

GOAL

Set water temperature to 120°F or the low setting; install a water heater blanket if you have an older heater.

CO2 CREDIT

Note: Check the box as you take each action.

❑ If you set your water heater thermostat at 120°F (between "low" and "medium" if your water heater doesn't show actual degrees) credit yourself 150 pounds of CO_2 annually.

❑ If you install an insulating blanket credit yourself 175 pounds of CO_2 annually.

❑ Bonus: If you have installed or plan to install a solar water heater in the next year, credit yourself 2,500 pounds of annual CO_2 savings.

12. LIGHT OF YOUR LIFE

Installing Energy Efficient Lights

WHY ACT?

The incandescent light bulb most of us use has been surpassed by the more durable and efficient compact fluorescent. It screws into regular light sockets and uses about 70% less electricity to provide the same amount of light as an old light bulb. While compact fluorescents (CFLs) cost more to buy than incandescents—about $6 to $20 per bulb—they use only about one-fourth the energy and will last about 10,000 hours compared with 1,000 for the typical incandescent bulb. This means they will last for about 8 years, but you will get your investment back in energy savings in about half that time. Using compact fluorescent light bulbs instead of incandescent bulbs in rooms where lights are on for at least 4 hours per day saves 100 pounds of CO_2 annually per bulb.

CO_2 REDUCTION ACTION

○ Do a room by room inventory of all your lighting fixtures that are on at least 3 hours a day. Make note of the wattage so you can purchase a compact fluorescent with equivalent lighting. As you do this inventory, look for opportunities to use only the lighting required for the task. Make sure you note which fixtures require dimmable or 3-way bulbs and which will be used outdoors (these require special CFLs).

○ Go to your local hardware store, home supply store, or green catalog and educate yourself about the choices.

○ Purchase and install the compact fluorescents needed for these rooms.

Note: Always turn off the lights when you leave the room and only light the parts of the room where you need it.

TIME & MATERIALS

○ An hour or two to complete your survey, and to purchase and install your new compact fluorescent light bulbs.

GOAL

Replace a minimum of 5 regular light bulbs with compact fluorescents in frequently used rooms.

CO₂ CREDIT

Note: Check the box as you take each action.

❑ Credit yourself 500 pounds of annual CO_2 savings for replacing 5 frequently used incandescent light bulbs with compact fluorescent light bulbs. Credit yourself 100 pounds for each additional frequently used light bulb replaced with a compact fluorescent.

Use this chart to keep track of incandescent bulbs you have changed to compact fluorescent bulbs. (Remember 3-way, dimmer, and outdoor sockets require special CFLs.)

Location of bulb	3-way	Dimmer	Outdoor	Installed ✓
_____	❑	❑	❑	❑
_____	❑	❑	❑	❑
_____	❑	❑	❑	❑
_____	❑	❑	❑	❑
_____	❑	❑	❑	❑
_____	❑	❑	❑	❑
_____	❑	❑	❑	❑
_____	❑	❑	❑	❑

Total bulbs installed: _____

❑ Credit yourself 100 pounds for each bulb installed
    100 X _____ = _____

13. CHILL OUT

Sealing Air Leaks

WHY ACT?

Air leaks around doors, windows, and electrical outlets; through the fireplace; in basements (between the foundation and the frame); and especially in attics lose as much heat, in the typical home, as leaving an average-size window open all winter long. The extra heating fuel required to compensate for these energy leaks represents up to 800 pounds of CO_2 emissions annually. This action will help you plug your CO_2 leaks.

CO_2 REDUCTION ACTION

○ Determine where to seal by checking your fireplace, feeling around doors, windows, electrical, and plumbing outlets, and cracks between the foundation and the frame of the house where cold air may be coming in. A candle or incense stick can help you locate these cold air leaks.

○ Purchase the following inexpensive items from your local hardware or home supply store and install where needed: weather stripping, outlet insulators, caulking, insulating foam, window putty, and door "sweeps." If you are a tenant, see if you can work out a plan with your landlord to deduct the cost of installation and materials from your rent.

TIME & MATERIALS

○ Up to an hour to do audit and another few hours for simple low-cost improvements.

○ Weather stripping, outlet insulators, caulking, insulating foam, window putty, and door "sweeps."

GOAL

Find and seal all energy leaks in your home.

CO_2 CREDIT

Note: Check the box as you take the action.

❑ For thoroughly sealing the air leaks in your home, credit yourself 800 pounds of annual CO_2 reduction.

14. FURNACE FLING

Tuning Up Your Furnace

WHY ACT?

One of the most important things you can do to save energy is to regularly tune up your furnace. Up to 50% of the energy you use in your home goes to heating it. And a heating system can waste up to 50% of the energy it uses if it's not operating efficiently. This can represent as much as 3,750 pounds of CO_2 wastefully going into the air each year.

CO2 REDUCTION ACTION

- Oil furnaces need a tune-up once a year; gas furnaces should get one every 2 years. The tune-up should cost about $75.

- Call your furnace servicing company and schedule an appointment to have your furnace cleaned and adjusted based on a combustion efficiency test.

- Seal all joints in your warm-air ducts with mastic or duct tape that meets UL-181 specifications (it will say on the package if it meets this standard).

- If your warm-air heating ducts that pass through unheated areas such as crawl spaces are not insulated, ask your technician to either include that as part of the servicing or show you how to do it. This can improve the efficiency of your heating system by as much as 30%.

TIME & MATERIALS

- 5 minutes to make an appointment, an hour or two to seal and insulate your warm air heating ducts.

- Phone, phone book, insulating materials.

GOAL

Tune up your furnace; seal and insulate warm-air heating ducts if needed.

CO2 CREDIT

Note: Check the box as you take each action.

❑ Credit yourself 300 pounds of CO_2 annually for a furnace tune-up.

❑ Credit yourself 800 pounds of CO_2 annually for sealing and insulating warm-air heating ducts.

❑ Bonus: Credit yourself 2,400 pounds of CO_2 reduction if you replace an old furnace with a new energy-efficient model in the next year.

15. A SUSTAINABLE ENERGY HOUSEHOLD
Achieving Maximum Energy Efficiency

WHY ACT?

Using energy efficiently is one of the major principles in creating a sustainable energy household. One starts by doing the easy and inexpensive things, such as remembering to turn off lights and appliances and taking the other energy efficiency actions already described. This action invites you to go farther down the path—achieving maximum energy efficiency. This action will pay for itself over time and could reduce your annual CO_2 emissions by several thousand pounds per year.

CO_2 REDUCTION ACTION

❍ Begin by becoming knowledgeable about where your house is on the path of energy efficiency by contacting an energy expert and getting an on-site audit. Audits may be provided by the utility that heats your home.

❍ Examine your major appliances. If the appliance has a yellow "Energy Guide" sticker, make a note of its annual energy use and compare it with new Energy Star® models in a showroom. Refrigerators and freezers have achieved dramatic improvements in efficiency over the last 10 years. If your refrigerator is more than 10 years old, a new Energy Star® refrigerator could reduce CO_2 emissions by more than 500 pounds per year.

❍ Based on what you learned from your research and audit, develop a 1–3 year plan of action for maximizing your home's energy efficiency. Develop full details for Year One including a budget and timeline. In calculating the cost/benefit of a particular energy efficiency option or renewable energy technology, consider the payback period, comfort, environmental impact, convenience, and current investment budget.

TIME & MATERIALS

❍ 5 or 6 hours—1 to 2 hours to locate and contact an energy expert, an hour or two to review the findings, a couple of hours to create your plan and commit to the first action.

❍ Paper, pen, telephone, yellow pages.

GOAL

Develop a multi-year plan for maximizing your home's energy efficiency and use of renewable energy. Commit to a Year One goal of reducing a minimum of 800 pounds of CO_2 through weatherizing some portion of your house (insulating attics, walls, or foundations; window replacement; or comprehensive weather stripping and leak sealing).

CO_2 CREDIT

Note: Check the box as you take each action.

❑ Credit yourself 1,200 pounds of annual CO_2 reduction for insulating your walls and attic within the next year.

❑ Credit yourself 800 pounds of CO_2 reduction for adding storm windows or installing high efficiency windows within the next year.

❑ Credit yourself 500 pounds of CO_2 reduction for replacing an older refrigerator with a new, Energy Star® model.

16. GREEN POWER

Switching to Renewable Energy

WHY ACT?

Ultimately, the key to reducing carbon dioxide is to shift from using fossil fuels to using renewable energy (wind, solar, small hydro, biomass). This form of energy reduces not only CO_2 emissions but also pollutants in the air. You can purchase "green power" from a local electrical utility company. While this source of energy is currently a little more expensive—\$3–\$5 per month—you can easily make up for the costs with the energy efficiency cost savings from the other actions in this program. This action is one of the most effortless ways to reduce your CO_2 emissions.

CO2 REDUCTION ACTION

- ○ Determine your annual kWh usage from your utility bills.
- ○ Contact your energy utility and find out how you can shift your electric energy to green power.
- ○ If you are unsuccessful in purchasing green power from your local utility, contact The Green Power Network at www.eere.energy.gov/greenpower to find out where it can be purchased.

Note: Consider taking this action all the way and becoming energy independent by installing solar or wind in your home. The costs are coming down with many states providing generous subsidies and installers developing innovative financing strategies. For more information about how to find an installation contractor in your area, visit www.findsolar.com, www.verdeenergy.com, or your local yellow pages.

TIME & MATERIALS

- ○ 30 minutes to read your utility bill and call your local energy provider.
- ○ Phone, paper, and pen.

GOAL

Shift your electric energy to green power.

CO2 CREDIT

Note: Check the box as you take the action.

❏ Credit your household 200 pounds of CO_2 reduction for each 100 kWh of green power you purchase.

17. Is Your Car Physically Fit?

Maintaining an Efficient Car

WHY ACT?

Every gallon of gasoline used generates approximately 20 pounds of CO_2. A tuned car improves fuel efficiency as much as 30%. This translates as a big opportunity for saving CO_2 and fuel costs. This action will help keep your car purring.

CO_2 REDUCTION ACTION

○ Have your car serviced on a regular basis.
  - Consult your car owner's manual for guidelines.
  - If you are due for service, make an appointment.

○ Buy a tire gauge and use it periodically.
  - Inflate your tires to the pressure that is printed on them.
  - Always check and adjust the pressure before the tires are too warm.

TIME & MATERIALS

○ 10 minutes to study the owner's manual, 5 minutes to make an appointment; a few minutes every now and then to check your tire pressure.

○ Car owner's manual and tire gauge.

GOAL

Tune up your car.

CO_2 CREDIT

Note: Check the box as you take the action.

❑ 1,500 pounds of CO_2 reduced annually for an engine tune-up and maintaining tire pressure.

18. BEFRIEND AN EARTH-SMART AUTO

Buying a Fuel-Efficient Car

WHY ACT?

If you are considering purchasing a new car in the near future, this is an important action for you. You can make a dramatic improvement in your CO_2 emissions and save a considerable amount of money in gasoline costs by purchasing a more fuel-efficient auto. The average car in America gets 22 mpg. Compare this to currently available models that get over 60 mpg! This action will help you befriend an Earth-smart auto.

CO_2 REDUCTION ACTION

○ At the dealer showroom, check the fuel economy label affixed to the window for the model's average mpg, estimated annual fuel cost, and the fuel economy range for other models in the same class. Compare the figures to those of other manufacturers using the Environmental Protection Agency's free gas mileage guide that dealers are required to provide, or you can find it on the internet at www.fueleconomy.gov.

○ Purchase the lightest vehicle you can, keeping in mind that every option adds weight. A 10% weight reduction improves mileage by nearly 7%. Studies have indicated that the design of a vehicle is more important in terms of safety than its weight and size.

TIME & MATERIALS

○ A Saturday afternoon or two.

GOAL

Commit to purchasing a fuel-efficient car within the next year.

CO₂ CREDIT

Note: Check the box as you take the action.

❑ To find your annual CO₂ savings from purchasing a more fuel-efficient car, find the fuel efficiency of your current car in the top row of the table below. Find the number of miles you drive annually in the first column. Follow the row and column you selected to find the annual CO₂ emissions for your car. Current car emissions _____.

❑ Follow the same procedure for a new car that gets higher mpg, and then subtract the emissions from this car from your current emissions to estimate annual CO₂ savings. Your CO₂ credit from purchasing a new fuel efficient car is _____.

Miles driven/year	15 mpg	20 mpg	25 mpg	30 mpg	35 mpg	40 mpg	45 mpg	50 mpg	60 mpg
5,000	6,666	5,000	4,000	3,333	2,857	2,500	2,222	2,000	1,667
7,500	10,000	7,500	6,000	5,000	4,286	3,750	3,333	3,000	2,500
10,000	13,333	10,000	8,000	6,667	5,714	5,000	4,444	4,000	3,333
12,500	16,667	12,500	10,500	8,333	7,143	6,250	5,556	5,000	4,167
15,000	20,000	15,000	12,000	10,000	8,571	7,500	6,667	6,000	5,550
20,000	26,667	20,000	16,000	13,333	11,429	10,000	8,889	8,000	6,667

19. Carbon Neutral

Neutralizing Your Carbon Dioxide Footprint

WHY ACT?

By reducing your CO_2 emissions by 5,000 or more pounds you have taken a major step forward in lowering your greenhouse gas footprint. There are those, however, who wish to go further and explore the frontier of what's possible. This action is for those people. You can reduce your footprint to zero by offsetting your CO_2 emissions.

CO₂ REDUCTION ACTION

○ Deduct the actions you have already taken from your initial audit to determine the amount of CO_2 you need to offset. Then select actions from the list below that will offset your remaining CO_2 emissions.
Amount of initial CO_2 audit
(from the calculator you filled out) _____.
Amount I've reduced _____
Amount I still need to offset _____.

○ Plant trees. A single tree will absorb one ton of carbon dioxide over its lifetime. Shade provided by trees can also reduce your air conditioning bill by 10–15%. Contact the following web sites for information on trees and planting: www.arborday.org; www.plant-trees.org.

○ Purchase carbon credits online. A number of organizations have created ways to help you offset your CO_2 emissions. For a list of criteria for evaluating carbon offsets, a ranking by an independent assessor and places to purchase them visit:
www.cleanair-coolplanet.org/ConsumersGuidetoCarbonOffsets.pdf.

○ Whenever you travel by air, purchase carbon offsets to compensate for the emissions associated with the air travel. See www.betterworldclub.com or www.flyneutral.org. Many travel agents and airlines also provide this travel service.

Note: To go beyond carbon neutral, help others reduce their emissions. The next section shows you how.

TIME & MATERIALS

Phone, paper, time or money to contribute.

GOAL

To neutralize your remaining household CO_2 emissions.

CO2 CREDIT

Note: Check the box as you take each action.

❑ The amount of CO_2 offsets needed to be carbon neutral = _____.

❑ Planting Trees. Number of trees planted x 25 pounds of CO_2 reduction per tree = _____ CO_2 credit.

❑ Carbon Credit offsets = _____ desired CO_2 credit to be carbon neutral.

❑ Carbon free air travel offsets = _____ desired CO_2 credit to neutralize travel.

THANK YOU

Section Three:
Empowering Others to Lose
Unwanted Pounds

20. Psst... Save the Planet, Pass It On

Encouraging People You Know to Go on a Low Carbon Diet

WHY ACT?

To make a dent in America's huge CO_2 emissions, we need to get many people to become part of the solution. Imagine each household that does this program successfully getting at least five other households to participate and each losing 5,000 pounds. Imagine that this cycle continues. Within a relatively short period of time, we would achieve an exponential reduction in CO_2 emissions. This action helps you contribute to this vision becoming a reality.

CO₂ REDUCTION ACTION

○ Go through your address book or e-mail list and identify all the people you know who might be receptive to lowering their CO_2 impact. When given the opportunity, most people want to do the right thing. Include family, friends, neighbors, co-workers, and members of your faith community, social network, and community group.

○ Determine your outreach approach. In person is the best, followed by a phone call. A personalized e-mail communication followed by a phone call is a good way to go if you wish to reach out to many people. Also consider enrolling organizations and networks who can get the word out to their members.

○ In your communication, tell the person why you chose to participate in the program, the results you achieved, and why you have invited them to participate. Make it as personal as possible. For individuals who choose not to participate, continue to be a good example. Watching you may encourage them to participate in the future.

○ If you have done this program as a team, a great way to get people involved is to invite them to an information meeting hosted by your team. At the meeting, encourage them to join a team and link them up. A meeting script is provided in the support section on page 57.

○ Support people who participate with a call or e-mail. Ask how they are doing and offer your assistance if they need any help. Being able to translate good intention into behavior change is bolstered by support.

Note: To take this further, consider hosting a Global Warming Café in your community. This is a powerful way to engage community members in a conversation about global warming and then translate their concern into action through participation in *Low Carbon Diet* EcoTeams. To learn more, visit www.empowermentinstitute.net/lcd.

TIME & MATERIALS

○ 5 to 10 minutes to connect with people you care about. A few minutes to follow-up. 90 minutes per information meeting.

○ List of people to invite, computer, internet, phone.

GOAL

Select the level you wish to achieve. Once you gain the experience and confidence achieving that level, consider challenging yourself to reach for the next level. To stay on track, set a timeframe for achieving your goal.

Low Carbon Diet Club

❏ Level 1: 25,000 Pound Club – 5 households participating in *Low Carbon Diet*.

❏ Level 2: 100,000 Pound Club – 20 households participating in *Low Carbon Diet*.

❏ Level 3: 250,000 Pound Club – 50 households participating in *Low Carbon Diet*.

❏ Level 4: 500,000 Pound Club – 100 households participating in *Low Carbon Diet*.

❏ Level 5: 1,000,000 Pound Club – 200 households or more participating in *Low Carbon Diet*.

Date goal will be achieved _____

CO₂ CREDIT

Credit yourself 5,000 pounds for each household you enroll to do the program.

By doing this action I helped reduce _____ pounds of CO_2.

21. A Cool Place to Work

Helping Your Workplace Reduce its CO_2 Footprint

WHY ACT?

Now that you have put your own house in order, it's natural to want to practice your CO_2 reduction practices all the time, including during work hours, assuming you work outside of the home. However, you may find that you are unable to continue your CO_2 reduction action at work, because there are no systems in place. Perhaps there is no recycling or it is not as complete as it could be. Maybe car pools have not been formed even though many of your co-workers live along the same route to work. Or perhaps no bike rack has been installed where people could park their bikes. This action will help your workplace become part of the global warming solution.

CO_2 REDUCTION ACTION

- Go back through this book and choose one or more actions you are unable to take at work because something needed is unavailable.

- Think through what needs to be done to make it possible to implement the action(s).

- Speak to your manager or employer, or if you are in charge, speak to your employees, and ask for their support. Volunteer your time to help bring the action(s) about.

TIME & MATERIALS

- Up to an hour to think about what needs to be done and speak to your manager or employees. Several hours to assist in carrying out the action.

- Whatever materials are needed to change your workplace.

GOAL

One or more actions from this workbook transferred to your workplace.

CO_2 CREDIT

Extrapolate the household CO_2 reduction number for the action(s) you transfer to your workplace.

By doing this action I helped reduce _____ pounds of CO_2.

43

22. A Cool Community

Empower Your Community to Go on a Low Carbon Diet

WHY ACT?

Imagine Americans coming together to do something about global warming. Imagine small and large groups gathering in our community centers, places of worship and town halls to speak their minds and hearts about the global crisis facing us, and taking action to turn it around. Imagine them being given the tools they need to reduce their own carbon footprints and the strategies to empower their communities to do the same. Imagine communities across the country engaged in a campaign, household by household, to reduce their carbon footprints 20% by 2010. Now imagine that your community is part of it!

CO2 REDUCTION ACTION

○ Team up with other interested individuals to host a Global Warming Café outreach event to seed EcoTeams and generate advocacy for a Cool Community campaign.

○ Visit Empowerment Institute's website at www.empowermentinstitute.net/lcd. Sign up for a free Cool Community Teletraining and learn how to launch a Cool Community Campaign and host a Global Warming Café. Or just use resources on the web site.

○ Calculate your community residential carbon footprint by multiplying the number of households by the average American footprint of 55,000 pounds. (In most communities, this represents 75% or more of the community carbon footprint.)

○ Meet with community elected officials – mayor or town supervisor as well as your council member. Ask them to consider co-sponsoring a Global Warming Café and launching a Cool Community campaign. Share your experience of reducing your own carbon footprint, your vision for the campaign and willingness to contribute your time.

○ Help your community roll out *Low Carbon Diet: A 30 Day Program to Lose 5,000 Pounds* to help achieve the 20% carbon reduction goal. Keep score as the reductions add up to sustain momentum for change.

TIME & MATERIALS

○ A day or two for your team to plan and host a Global Warming Café. If you participate directly, a long-term dedication of service to your community and planet.

○ Computer, internet and phone. Good community organizing skills if you are helping manage the campaign.

GOAL

Select the level you wish to accomplish. Once your community gains the experience and confidence achieving that level, challenge it to reach for the next level. To stay on track, set a timeframe for achieving your goal.

Cool Community Campaign Levels

❑ Level 1: 5 Million Pounds – 1,000 households participate in *Low Carbon Diet*.
❑ Level 2: 25 Million Pounds – 5,000 households participate in *Low Carbon Diet*.
❑ Level 3: 50 Million Pounds – 10,000 households participate in *Low Carbon Diet*.
❑ Level 4: 100 Million Pounds – 20,000 households participate in *Low Carbon Diet*.
❑ Level 5: 250 Million Pounds – 50,000 households participate in *Low Carbon Diet*
❑ Level 6: 500 Million Pounds – 100,000 households participate in *Low Carbon Diet*.
❑ Level 7: 1 Billion Pounds – 200,000 or more households participate in *Low Carbon Diet*

Date goal will be achieved _____

CO_2 CREDIT

Credit yourself 5,000 pounds for each household in your community that participates. If you do this action as a team, divide up the CO_2 credits and also add a lifetime supply of goodwill from your community and planet.

By doing this action I helped reduce _____ pounds of CO_2.

45

23. A COOL CITIZEN

Helping Your Community Set Up CO$_2$ Reduction Systems

WHY ACT?

As you participated in this program, there may have been actions you would have taken if only the support existed in your community. You might have recycled certain items if your recycling center had accepted them. Maybe you would have bicycled to work if your community had safe bike lanes. And if public transportation were better, you might have been able to leave your car at home more often. This action will help you engage your government officials in developing municipal systems that can lower citizens' CO$_2$ footprints. If your community has decided to do a Cool Community Campaign, this action will help citizens more easily achieve their CO$_2$ reduction goals.

CO$_2$ REDUCTION ACTION

- Go back through this book and select actions you were unable to take or take as far as you wanted because what you needed wasn't available in your community.

- Think through what would need to be done and develop a proposal for how it might get implemented. Estimate as best as you can the CO$_2$ reduction savings when this system is utilized by citizens (provide a low, medium and high usage). Also add financial benefits to the municipality, where possible, to offset the investment. Solicit the ideas of knowledgeable government officials or community groups in putting together your proposal.

- When you have created your proposal, set up a meeting with your local government official to discuss it.

- When you meet with your local official, talk about your experience of the program, the results you achieved, and your proposal. Ask for his or her leadership to spearhead this initiative for your community. Indicate your willingness to contribute your time to this endeavor.

- It takes perseverance to build momentum for local government change. Stay with it and continue your advocacy until you make it happen.

Note: Stay tuned to CO$_2$ reduction legislation at the local, state, and national levels. Contact your elected official and let them know that you are doing your part and either thank them or encourage them to do their part.

TIME & MATERIALS

○ Depending on the complexity of the proposal, several hours to a few days to develop it. An hour to meet with municipal officials. Several hours on a regular basis to advocate for the proposal.

○ Phone number of local elected or government official. Computer, internet, and phone.

GOAL

To help your community establish a CO_2 reduction system(s) to enable residents to lower their footprint.

CO_2 CREDIT

Use the CO_2 reduction estimate in your proposal. When implemented, refine based on participation studies.

By doing this action I helped reduce _____ pounds of CO_2.

24. A Cool School

Helping Children Adopt Environmentally Sustainable Lifestyles

WHY ACT?

Along with doing your part to reduce the climate crisis future generations will inherit, you can also pass on knowledge about how to be part of the solution. This action provides a school curriculum to help students reduce their CO_2 footprint by taking many of the actions in the *Low Carbon Diet* program. Thousands of students in hundreds of schools around America have participated in this program. This action will help ensure that the future will be in able hands.

CO_2 REDUCTION ACTION

○ Learn about the *Journey for the Planet* school curriculum by visiting www.empowermentinstitute.net/lcd.

○ Set up an appointment with a teacher, youth program leader, principal, or superintendent.

○ When you meet, talk about your experience of the *Low Carbon Diet* program, the results you achieved, and your vision for why you wish the school to participate in the *Journey for the Planet* program. Ask for his or her leadership to spearhead this for the school. Indicate your willingness to contribute your time to this endeavor as needed.

○ It will take perseverance to get this in motion. Stay with it and continue your advocacy until you make it happen.

Note: Consider using *Journey for the Planet* to help children in your life lower their carbon footprint.

TIME & MATERIALS

○ A few hours to prepare and meet with school or youth organization representative.

○ Phone number of person you need to meet with. Computer, internet, and phone.

GOAL

To introduce this program into a local school(s) or youth program(s).

CO2 CREDIT

One of the most important long-term solutions to the global warming crisis is helping children adopt environmentally sustainable lifestyle practices that they can maintain over their lifetime. In the short-term, credit yourself with 500 pounds for each child who participates in the program. Over the long-term, you are helping to secure a sustainable future for our planet.

By doing this action I helped reduce _____ pounds of CO_2.

Section Four:
CO₂ Reduction Action Plans

CO₂ REDUCTION ACTION PLANS

Use the action plan charts on the next three pages to calculate your CO_2 reduction action plan. Determine the actions you wish to take that equal 5,000 pounds or greater. When you have completed your overall action plan transfer the results to the summary chart below.

Note: The CO_2 reduction values assigned to actions are approximations based on national averages and other broad assumptions.

CO_2 reduction goal _____

SUMMARY RESULTS OF ACTIONS TAKEN AND PLEDGED		
Write totals from action plans in the boxes below.		
	Pounds reduced by end of program	Pounds reduction pledged for future
SECTION ONE		
SECTION TWO		
SECTIONS ONE AND TWO TOTAL		
SECTION THREE PLEDGES		

SECTION ONE: COOL LIFESTYLE ACTION PLAN

ACTIONS	Pounds you can lose annually by doing this action	Will do action	Action Done	Pounds reduced by end of program	Pounds reduction pledged for future	Date I will complete this action
1. DUMPING ON GARBAGE – Reducing Solid Waste						
Reducing solid waste (see table on page 8)	1560 – 3120 pounds	☐	☐	_____	_____	_____
Recycling curbside 100%	1300 pounds	☐	☐	_____	_____	_____
2. AM I CLEAN YET? – Reducing Hot Water Used in Showers						
Install low-flow shower heads	250 pounds	☐	☐	_____	_____	_____
Reduce shower times to 5 minutes	300 lbs/person	☐	☐	_____	_____	_____
3. SCRUB-A-DUB TUB – Reducing Water Used for Washing Dishes						
Reduce electric dishwasher use per week	100 lbs/ea. load less	☐	☐	_____	_____	_____
Adopt sustainable hand-dishwashing habits	125 pounds	☐	☐	_____	_____	_____
Purchase an Energy Star® dishwasher	125 pounds	☐	☐	_____	_____	_____
4. WEAR IT AGAIN SAM – Washing and Drying Clothes Efficiently						
Reducing warm or hot wash loads per week	100 lbs/ea. load less	☐	☐	_____	_____	_____
Reducing number of weekly dryer loads	260 lbs/ea. load less	☐	☐	_____	_____	_____
Purchase an Energy Star® front load washer	500 pounds	☐	☐	_____	_____	_____
5. BETTER A SWEATER – Turning Down the Heating Thermostat						
Set thermostat to 65-68 when people are home and active; set it to 55-58 at night and when no one is home	1400 pounds	☐	☐	_____	_____	_____
6. PLUG YOUR ELECTRICITY LEAKS – Turning Your Appliances All the Way Off	600 pounds	☐	☐	_____	_____	_____
7. CHILL-IN – Cooling More Efficiently						
Replace or clean AC filter as recommended	350 pounds	☐	☐	_____	_____	_____
Raise your thermostat 4 degrees	60-240 pounds	☐	☐	_____	_____	_____
Purchase an Energy Star® air conditioner	600 pounds	☐	☐	_____	_____	_____
8. THINK BEFORE YOU GO – Reducing Vehicle Miles Traveled						
Reduce miles driven in a car or truck by 20%	450-4000 pounds	☐	☐	_____	_____	_____
9. DRIVE EARTH SMART – Fuel Efficient Driving	1100 lbs/ vehicle	☐	☐	_____	_____	_____
10. CHEW ON THIS FOR A WHILE – Eating Lower on the Food Chain						
Switch from meat to vegetarian meals one or more days a week	700 pounds for each regular day switched	☐	☐	_____	_____	_____
TOTALS (transfer to summary page)						

SECTION TWO: COOL HOUSEHOLD SYSTEMS ACTION PLAN

ACTIONS	Pounds you can lose annually by doing this action	Will do action	Action Done	Pounds reduced by end of program	Pounds reduction pledged for future	Date I will complete this action
11. MEET YOUR WATER HEATER – Making Your Water Heater Efficient						
Set temperature of your water heater to 120°	150 pounds	☐	☐	_____	_____	_____
Insulating your hot water heater	175 pounds	☐	☐	_____	_____	_____
Installing a solar hot water heater	2500 pounds	☐	☐	_____	_____	_____
12. LIGHT OF YOUR LIFE – Installing Energy Efficient Lights						
Installing five compact fluorescent bulbs	500 pounds	☐	☐	_____	_____	_____
Installing additional compact fluorescent bulbs	100 lbs/ bulb	☐	☐	_____	_____	_____
13. CHILL OUT – Sealing Air Leaks						
Thoroughly sealing air leaks in your home	800 pounds	☐	☐	_____	_____	_____
14. FURNACE FLING - Tune Up Your Furnace						
Furnace tune-up	300 pounds	☐	☐	_____	_____	_____
Sealing and insulating warm-air heating ducts	800 pounds	☐	☐	_____	_____	_____
Purchasing an energy-efficient furnace	2400 pounds	☐	☐	_____	_____	_____
15. A SUSTAINABLE ENERGY HOUSEHOLD – Achieving Maximum Energy Efficiency						
Insulating your walls and attic	1200 pounds	☐	☐	_____	_____	_____
Installing storm or high-efficiency windows	800 pounds	☐	☐	_____	_____	_____
Replace old refrigerator with a new, Energy Star® model	500 pounds	☐	☐	_____	_____	_____
16. GREEN POWER – Switching to Renewable Energy						
Purchasing "green power" from electric utility	200 lbs per 100 kWh	☐	☐	_____	_____	_____
17. IS YOUR CAR PHYSICALLY FIT? - Maintaining an Efficient Car						
Engine tune-up and maintaining air-pressure in your tires	1500 pounds	☐	☐	_____	_____	_____
18. BEFRIEND AN EARTH-SMART AUTO – Buying a Fuel-Efficient Car						
Purchase a more fuel-efficient vehicle than you currently drive	2000–10,000 lbs	☐	☐	_____	_____	_____
19. CARBON NEUTRAL – Neutralizing Your Carbon Dioxide Footprint						
Planting trees	25 pounds/tree	☐	☐	_____	_____	_____
Purchasing carbon offsets	As much as you like	☐	☐	_____	_____	_____
Purchasing travel offsets	As much as you want	☐	☐	_____	_____	_____
TOTALS (transfer to summary page)						

Section Three: Empowering Others to Lose Unwanted Pounds Action Plan

ACTIONS	Pounds you can lose annually by doing this action	Will do action	Action Done	Pounds reduced by end of program	Pounds reduction pledged for future	Date I will complete this action
20. PSST...SAVE THE PLANET, PASS IT ON – Encouraging People You Know to Go on a *Low Carbon Diet*.						
Level 1: 5 Households	25,000 pounds	☐	☐	_____	_____	_____
Level 2: 20 Households	100,000 pounds	☐	☐	_____	_____	_____
Level 3: 50 Households	250,000 pounds	☐	☐	_____	_____	_____
Level 4: 100 Households	500,000 pounds	☐	☐	_____	_____	_____
Level 5: 200 Households	1,000,000 pounds	☐	☐	_____	_____	_____
21. A COOL PLACE TO WORK – Helping Your Workplace Reduce its CO_2 Footprint	_____ pounds	☐	☐	_____	_____	_____
22. A COOL COMMUNITY – Helping Your Community Go on a *Low Carbon Diet*						
Level 1: 1,000 Households	5 Million pounds	☐	☐	_____	_____	_____
Level 2: 5,000 Households	25 Million pounds	☐	☐	_____	_____	_____
Level 3: 10,000 Households	50 Million pounds	☐	☐	_____	_____	_____
Level 4: 20,000 Households	100 Million pounds	☐	☐	_____	_____	_____
Level 5: 50,000 Households	250 Million pound	☐	☐	_____	_____	_____
Level 6: 100,000 Households	500 Million pounds	☐	☐	_____	_____	_____
Level 7: 200,000 Households	1 Billion pounds	☐	☐	_____	_____	_____
23. A COOL CITIZEN – Helping Your Community Set Up CO_2 Reduction Systems						
Community proposal reduction goal _____	_____ pounds	☐	☐	_____	_____	_____
24. A COOL SCHOOL – Helping Children Adopt Environmentally Sustainable Lifestyles						
Number of students participating _____	500 pounds/student	☐	☐	_____	_____	_____
TOTALS (transfer to summary page)						

ACTION PLAN NOTES

Section Five:
Program Support Tools

INTRODUCTION

This section provides a support structure to help you effectively implement the program. It includes:

Team Initiator Guidelines: A 5-step process for starting your team.

Information Meeting Guide: A script for conducting an informational meeting for potential team members. It is also possible to use elements for one-on-one communications.

Team-Building Meeting Guide: A script for conducting the first team meeting. This team can consist of household members or 5 to 8 friends, neighbors, colleagues, or faith community members. The focus of the meeting is to create a support system, learn how to calculate your CO_2 footprint and develop your action plan to reduce it.

Topic Meeting Guides: These scripts are for meetings 2 to 4. The goal in these meetings is for team participants to report on actions taken, describe action plans for the next section, and get support.

TEAM INITIATOR GUIDELINES

1. If you are starting the team, you are the team initiator. To learn about the program, read the introduction, how the program works, the table of contents and review the actions.

2. Set a date and time for hosting a Team Building Meeting either in your home or at some other location.

3. Create your team. This can consist of family, friends, neighbors, co-workers, or members of your faith community or civic organization. Choose the community that is easiest to pull together. The best size for a team is 5–8 households. If that is not possible, your household unit can become the team. If potential team members wish to know more about the program, invite them to visit www.empowermentinstitute.net/lcd.

4.. Each household will need to have a copy of this book. It can be purchased on-line at www.empowermentinstitute.net/lcd. Quantity discounts start at 20 books. Books can also be purchased from Amazon.com, your local bookstore, or from a participating organization.

5. You are responsible for leading the 4 meetings. Meeting scripts are located in Section Five, Program Support Tools. Before the Team Building Meeting, review the script, calculate your CO_2 footprint at www.empowermentinstitute.net/lcd and create your CO_2 reduction action plan on pages 51 to 54.

INFORMATION MEETING GUIDE

BEFORE EVENT

○ If possible, serve light refreshments and set up room in a U shape to increase sense of intimacy.

○ Review this script before the meeting so that you are familiar with the process.

AGENDA (Times Approximate)

1. Welcome, Purpose, Agenda – 10 minutes
2. Introductions – 15 minutes
3. Overview of Challenge – 15 minutes
4. Program Description – 10 minutes
5. Q & A – 15 minutes
6. Invitation to Participate – 10 minutes
7. Sign-up – 15 minutes
Total Time: 90 minutes

1. Welcome, Purpose, Agenda – 10 minutes

○ Welcome: Welcome and appreciate people for coming. State your name and role as the team initiator.

○ Purpose: To provide an opportunity to be part of the global warming solution. Add your personal motivation for organizing this event.

○ Agenda: Introductions, overview of challenge, program description, Q & A, invitation to participate.

2. Introductions – 15 minutes

○ Invite participants to state name, where they live, and any other important information and to say what they would like out of the meeting. If a large group limit the sharing to 8-10 people.

3. Overview of Challenge – 15 minutes

○ Read out key passages from the Introduction.

○ If people have seen Al Gore's movie "An Inconvenient Truth," invite to comment briefly on their experience.

○ *Low Carbon Diet* Vision: Empowering Americans to become leaders in addressing the global warming issue.

4. Program Description – 10 minutes

○ Show copy of this book and read "How the Program Works"

5. Q & A – 15 minutes

○ Invite questions about the program and their participation. Draw out any concerns that individuals might have about participation.

6. Invitation to Participate on a Team – 10 minutes

○ Ask how many are interested in participating in the program? Acknowledge those that raise their hand and draw out any concerns from those who didn't. For those who can't join now, invite them to do the program on their own or join a team in the future.

○ Invite participants to spread the word to others and have them contact you if they wish to participate on a team. Provide your name, e-mail, and phone number on a flip chart if available.

7. Team Program Sign Up and Placement – 15 minutes

○ If several teams are formed, organize in groups of 5–8 households by proximity, affinity, or other criteria.

○ All can meet at one location and then divide up into sub-groups of 5–8 households or can divide up into separate teams. In either case, request a volunteer from each team to serve as team leader. Point them to the scripts starting on page 59 of the book that tell them how to lead the meetings.

○ Set date(s) for the Team Building Meeting.

TEAM BUILDING MEETING GUIDE

BEFORE EVENT

- Calculate your household CO_2 footprint in advance of the meeting so you can share it, and answer any questions your team might have about the process. Use the LCD calculator at www.empowermentinstitute.net/lcd.

- Decide on your goal for the program and create your CO_2 Reduction Action Plan (pages 51–54) to share at the meeting.

- Review this guide before the meeting so you are familiar with the process.

AGENDA (Times Approximate)

1. Welcome, Purpose, Overview – 15 minutes
2. Participants State Reasons for Joining – 20 minutes
3. Review How Program Works – 10 minutes
4. Review CO_2 Calculator – 10 minutes
5. Review Workbook and Action Plan – 20 minutes
6. Schedule Meetings – 15 minutes
7. Next Steps – 5 minutes
Total Time – 1.5 to 2 Hours

1. Welcome, Purpose, Overview – 15 minutes

- Welcome participants and thank them for coming. State why you were motivated to form this team.

- Indicate that the purpose of this meeting is to learn how to calculate our CO_2 footprint, create a plan to reduce it, and develop a support system to help us carry it out.

- Review highlights from the introduction to the book on page 1.

2. Participants State Reasons for Participating – 20 minutes

- Ask team members to state their name, where they live (if relevant), and why they chose to participate.

- Write down why each person chose to participate.

- At the end, summarize the key reasons individuals chose to participate. Create into a team statement of purpose. Invite team members to write this in their book.

3. Review How Program Works – 10 minutes

○ Review five points on page 5.

4. Review CO_2 Calculator – 10 minutes

○ Share your CO_2 calculation printout.

○ Share with the team what you learned from doing your calculation.

○ Answer any questions they may have about doing this.

5. Review Workbook and Action Plan – 20 minutes

○ Invite an individual to read aloud the actions in the table of contents to familiarize the team with the program content.

○ Review the format of one action from each of the three sections.

○ Share your numerical CO_2 reduction goal and action plan to achieve it.

○ Answer any questions about this process.

6. Schedule Meetings – 15 minutes

○ Schedule the next 3 meetings, allowing 10–14 days between meetings to take the actions.

○ Request that everyone commit to coming on time and you will commit to ending within 2 hours of the start time.

○ If something unexpected occurs and someone cannot attend a meeting, request that the person notify you in advance and provide you with their action plan. You will call them after the meeting to let them know what happened.

7. Review Next Steps – 5 minutes

○ Go to www.empowermentinstitute.net/lcd and fill in the calculator to determine your CO_2 footprint. Bring the printout of your results to the next meeting. If you don't have access to the internet, and are unable to do a CO_2 calculation of current use, simply proceed with the next step.

○ Determine your CO_2 reduction goal and create your overall action plan.

○ Read through this workbook and choose the actions you and your household will take to achieve your goal.

○ Fill out the CO_2 Reduction Action Plan on pages 51–54 of the workbook and bring it to the next meeting along with any request you may have for support.

TOPIC MEETING ONE GUIDE:
COOL LIFESTYLE PRACTICES

BEFORE MEETING

○ Read this meeting guide carefully and plan in advance what you will do for agenda items 1, 3, and 4.

○ Do the *Low Carbon Diet* actions you wish to demonstrate.

AGENDA (Times Approximate)

1. Inspirational Start – 5 minutes
2. Share CO_2 Footprint and Reduction Goal – 25 minutes
3. Demonstrate Action(s) – 15 minutes
4. Share CO_2 Reduction Action Plans – 30 minutes
5. Check-In on Team Performance – 10 minutes
6. Set Up Support Calls – 5 minutes
7. Review Next Steps – 5 minutes
8. Acknowledge Team's Accomplishments – 10 minutes
Total Time: 1.5 to 2 Hours

1. Inspirational Start – 5 minutes

○ Start with a brief poem, quote, personal anecdote, or something that connects the group to the meaning and larger purpose of what you are doing.

2. Share CO_2 Footprints and Reduction Goals – 25 minutes

○ Have each household share their CO_2 footprint and reduction goal. Invite reflection from individuals regarding this exercise.

3. Demonstrate Action(s) – 15 minutes

○ Demonstrate one or more actions you think might be helpful to the team. Show what you did and how you did it so the team can learn from your hands-on experience.

4. Share CO_2 Reduction Action Plans – 30 minutes

○ Explain that the actions in Section One require behavior change and then ongoing daily practice.

○ Read out each action from the Action Plan for Section One on page 48. Explain action if it needs any elaboration. Ask who plans to do that action including yourself.

○ Ask teammates to request support for carrying out any action they find challenging, for example, technical assistance, advice, or information. Encourage team members to offer support where they feel competent.

5. Check-In on Team Performance – 10 minutes

○ At each meeting take a little time to look at how the team is functioning and tune up as needed. A team that is committed to mutual accountability achieves the best CO_2 reduction results from this peer-support system.

○ If anyone did not come with their CO_2 calculation or CO_2 Reduction Action Plan, ask that household what happened and if they need any support in carrying it out. If they just did not get around to doing it, kindly ask if they will be able to bring it to the next meeting.

○ If any team members came late, request that they come on time in the future so the meeting can be run without interruptions. If a number of people came late, requiring you to delay the start of the meeting, request that they come on time so you can end on time. If people can't get there at the agreed upon time, ask if people would like to start the meeting later.

○ If anyone did not attend, call and ask the person if he/she is still committed to participating in the program. If so, request the person prioritize attending the following meetings. Explain what happened at this meeting.

6. Set Up Support Calls – 5 minutes

○ *Approximately half way between this meeting and the next, you as team leader are encouraged to call team members to see how they are doing in implementing their action plans. Left on our own, our motivation often wanes. These support calls make a big difference in assisting team members to stay on track.*

○ Arrange mutually convenient times for checking in with team members. Allow up to 10 minutes per call. If person is not there for the agreed upon call, leave a message and request a call back with a status report.

7. Review Next Steps – 5 minutes

○ Take the *Low Carbon Diet* actions you planned. Complete any incomplete actions from the previous meeting.

○ Read over the next topic's actions and fine tune your action plan if needed. Determine any support you wish from the team to implement it.

○ Bring your CO$_2$ Reduction Action Plan to the meeting to discuss with the team.

8. Acknowledge Team's Accomplishments – 10 minutes

○ Express your appreciation to team members for what they have accomplished. State in a sentence or two what was most meaningful for you and invite others to do the same. If appropriate, end with some type of celebration.

Topic Meeting Two Guide: Cool Household Practices

BEFORE MEETING

- Read this meeting guide carefully and plan in advance what you will do for items 1, 3, and 4.

- Do the *Low Carbon Diet* actions you wish to demonstrate.

AGENDA (Times Approximate)

1. Inspirational Start – 5 minutes
2. Share Actions Taken – 25 minutes
3. Demonstrate Action(s) – 15 minutes
4. Share Action Plans – 30 minutes
5. Check-In on Team Performance – 10 minutes
6. Set Up Support Calls – 5 minutes
7. Review Next Steps – 5 minutes
8. Acknowledge Team's Accomplishments – 10 minutes
9. Total Time: 1.5 to 2 Hours

1. Inspirational Start – 5 minutes

- Start with a brief poem, personal anecdote, or something that connects the group to the meaning and larger purpose of what you are doing.

2. Share Actions Taken – 25 minutes

- Have each household answer the following questions.

  1. What actions did you take?

  2. What did you learn?

  3. Where, if anywhere, did you encounter a problem and how did you address it?

  4. What support, if any, do you wish from the team?

3. Demonstrate Action(s) – 15 minutes

- Demonstrate one or more actions you think might be helpful to the team. Show what you did and how you did it so the team can learn from your hands-on experience.

4. Share Action Plans – 30 minutes

○ Explain that the actions in Section Two require system level changes. Many of these actions take no time at all and simply require turning a thermostat dial, others require securing the services of a professional, and some require purchasing products.

○ Read out each action from the Action Plan for Section Two on page 49. Explain action if it needs any elaboration. Ask who plans to do that action including yourself.

○ Ask teammates to request support for carrying out any action they find challenging, for example, technical assistance, advice, or information. Encourage team members to offer support where they feel competent.

5. Check-In on Team Performance – 10 minutes

○ If individuals did not take the actions they had planned, ask if the team can be helpful in supporting them to carry it out. If they did not get around to doing it, kindly ask if they will be able to take the actions before the next meeting.

○ If any team members came late, request that they come on time in the future so the meeting can be run without interruptions. If a number of people came late, requiring you to delay the start of the meeting, request that they come on time so you can end on time. If people can't get there at the agreed upon time, determine if you should start the meeting later.

○ If anyone did not attend, call and ask person if he/she is still committed to participating in the program. If so, request the person attend the following meetings. Explain what happened at this meeting.

6. Set Up Support Calls – 5 minutes

○ *Approximately half way between this meeting and the next, you as team leader are encouraged to call team members to see how they are doing in implementing their action plans. Left on our own, our motivation often wanes—these calls make a big difference in assisting team members to stay on track.*

○ Arrange mutually convenient times for checking in with team members. Allow up to 10 minutes per call.

7. Review Next Steps – 5 minutes

○ Take the *Low Carbon Diet* actions you planned. Complete any incomplete actions from the previous meeting.

○ Read over the next topic's actions and fine tune your action plan if needed. Determine any support you wish from the team to implement it.

○ Bring your Action Plan to the meeting to discuss with the team.

8. Acknowledge Team's Accomplishments – 10 minutes

○ Express your appreciation to team members for what they have accomplished. State in a sentence or two what was most meaningful for you and invite others to do the same. If appropriate, end with some type of celebration.

TOPIC MEETING THREE GUIDE: EMPOWERING OTHERS TO LOSE UNWANTED POUNDS

BEFORE MEETING

○ Read this meeting guide carefully and plan in advance what you will do for steps 1, 3, and 4 of the meeting agenda.

○ Make support calls to team members and remind them to complete their Action Plans and bring them to the meeting.

○ Do the *Low Carbon Diet* Empowering Others action(s) you wish to demonstrate.

AGENDA (Times Approximate)

1. Inspirational Start – 5 minutes
2. Share Actions Taken – 25 minutes
3. Fill in Program Summary Results - 10 minutes
4. Demonstrate Action(s) – 10 minutes
5. Share Action Plans – 20 minutes
6. Closure and Celebration – 30 minutes
Total Time: 1.5 to 2 Hours

1. Inspirational Start – 5 minutes

○ Start with a brief poem, quote, personal anecdote, or something that connects the group to the meaning and larger purpose of what you are doing.

2. Share Actions Taken – 25 minutes

○ Have each household answer the following questions:

1. What actions did you take?

2. What did you learn?

3. Where, if anywhere, did you encounter a problem and how did you address it?

4. What support, if any, do you wish from the team?

3. Fill in Program Summary Results – 10 minutes

○ Have each household transpose the results from their Action Plan to the Summary Results sheet in the workbook (page 51).

○ Fill in the pledges for future actions.

○ Be prepared to share results at the end of the meeting.

4. Demonstrate Action(s) – 10 minutes

○ Demonstrate one or more actions you think might be helpful to the team. Describe what you did and how you did it so the team can learn from your hands-on experience.

5. Share Action Plans – 20 minutes

○ Explain that the actions in Section Three focus on how to get others involved in reducing their CO_2 footprint. Explain that many of these actions will take a commitment of time and require some organizational skills.

○ Read out each action from the Action Plan for Section Three on page 50. Explain action if it needs any elaboration. Ask who plans to do that action, including yourself.

○ Ask teammates to request support for carrying out any action they find challenging, for example technical assistance, advice, or information. Encourage team members to offer support where they feel competent. If people wish to work together on actions, take time to arrange next steps

6. Closure and Celebration – 30 minutes.

○ Have each household share their Summary Results and as they give their results do a team tally.

○ Express your appreciation to team members for what they have accomplished.

○ Ask each person to state what they found most valuable about this experience.

○ End with a celebration.

SOURCES

Changing the World One Household at a Time: Portland's 30 Day Program to Lose 5000 Pounds, Sarah Juniper Rabkin and David Gershon, from the anthology, *Creating a Climate for Change: Communicating Climate Change – Facilitating Social Change*, Cambridge University Press, 2006

Denison, Richard (1996). *Environmental Life-Cycle Comparison of Recycling, Landfilling, and Incineration*, Annual Review of Energy and Environment: www.edf.org

Energy Information Administration (1999). 1997 Residential Energy Consumption Survey: www.eia.doe.gov/emeu/recs/.

Environmental Defense, *Undo It, 20 Simple Steps to Undo Global Warming*, www.undoit.org.

Gore, Albert (2006). *An Inconvenient Truth*, book and movie to educate citizens about global warming. www.climatecrisis.net.

Heede, Rick (1999). *Household Opportunities to Cool Global Warming*, Rocky Mountain Institute.

ICF (1999). Emissions Factors, Global Warming Potentials, Unit Conversions, Emissions, and Related Facts. Compiled by ICF Consulting, November 1999.

Lawrence Berkeley National Laboratory (2001). *The 20 Percent Solution*: http://savepower.lbl.gov/index.html.

NW Natural (2000). 2000 Integrated Resource Plan.

Oak Ridge National Laboratory (1999). Transportation Energy Data Book 20: http://www.ornl.gov/

Portland General Electric (2001). UE-115 Rate Case filed with Oregon Public Utilities Commission. *Updated Forecast of Residential Use per Occupied Account and Ultimate Deliveries,* PGE Exhibit 2205, Rebuttal Testimony and Exhibits.

Sullivan, G.P., J.W. Currie, T.C. Hillman, and G.B. Parker (2000). *Southern California Edison High-Performance Clothes Washer Demonstration at Leisure World Laguna Woods, Final Report*. Prepared for Southern California Edison by Pacific Northwest Laboratory: www.pnl.gov.

Sullivan, G.P., D.B. Elliott, T.C. Hillman, and A.R. Hadley (2001). *The Save Water and Energy Education Program: SWEEP Water and Energy Savings Evaluation*. Prepared for the U.S. Department of Energy by Pacific Northwest Laboratory: www.pnl.gov.

Trees for the Future, *The Global Cooling Answer Book*, Second edition, 2005. www.plant-trees.org

U.S. Department of Energy (1999). *Electric Power Annual*: www.eia.doe.gov/cneaf/electricity/epav1/epav1.html.

U.S. Environmental Protection Agency and Department of Energy (2001a). *Regular Maintenance Improves Gas Mileage*: http://www.fueleconomy.gov/feg/maintain.shtml.

U.S. Environmental Protection Agency and Department of Energy (2001b). *Tips to Improve Your Gas Mileage*: http://www.fueleconomy.gov/feg/drive.shtml.

Wilson and Morrill (1999). *Consumer Guide to Home Energy Savings*. 7th edition. American Council for an Energy-Efficiency Economy.

ABOUT THE AUTHOR

 David Gershon, founder and CEO of Empowerment Institute, is one of the world's leading authorities on behavior change and large-scale transformation. He applies his expertise to various issues requiring community, organizational, or societal transformation. His clients range from large cities and organizations to social entrepreneurs and transformational small businesses. He has addressed issues ranging from environmental behavior change to emergency preparedness; from organizational talent development to low-income neighborhood revitalization. Longitudinal research studies indicate that adopted behavior changes are sustained over time.

He conceived and organized, in partnership with the United Nations Children's Fund and ABC Television, one of the planet's first major global initiatives, the First Earth Run. At the height of the Cold War, using the mythic power of relaying fire around the world, millions of people, in partnership with the world's political leaders and media, participated in creating a profound sense of our connectedness.

David is the author of nine books including the bestselling *Empowerment: The Art of Creating Your Life As You Want It*, which has become a classic on the subject. He is currently writing *Changing the Game: A New Social Change Formula*. Considered a master personal development trainer, he co-directs the Empowerment Institute Certification Program, a school for transformative change. He has lectured at Harvard, MIT, and Duke and served as an advisor to the Clinton White House and United Nations on behavior change and sustainability issues. His work has received considerable media attention and many honors.

For more information visit www.empowermentinstitute.net. David can be contacted at dgershon@empowermentinstitute.net.

LOW CARBON DIET RESOURCES

Host a Global Warming Café – Based on the successful "World Café" group discussion format, this 4-hour workshop engages participants in a heartfelt conversation about global warming and then invites them to take personal action to reduce their carbon footprint using the tools in *Low Carbon Diet*. Those participants wishing to go further are invited to start a Cool Community Campaign to reduce their community's carbon footprint 20% by 2010. *The Global Warming Café Organizers Toolkit* is available for free online and provides everything you need to host and promote your Café. www.empowermentinstitute.net/lcd

Attend a FREE "Cool Community Teletraining" – For those interested in empowering their community to be part of the global warming solution, this two-hour training is an opportunity to learn key community empowerment strategies from *Low Carbon Diet* author David Gershon, who has dedicated his life to mastering and teaching them. Visit the Empowerment Institute website to register. www.empowermentinstitute.net/lcd

Empowerment Institute Certification Program: The Practice of Empowerment and Global Warming – Empowerment Institute has developed a highly successful set of tools for environmental behavior change and community empowerment. Over the past two decades, it has used these tools to help several hundred thousand people in hundreds of communities throughout the world reduce their environmental footprint by 25%. For those who desire more formal training in how to help communities or individuals reduce their carbon footprint, Empowerment Institute offers two certification opportunities: Its Cool Community Leadership Program and *Low Carbon Diet* Coaching Program. To learn more about the Empowerment Institute Certification Program visit www.empowermentinstitute.net.

Fundraise for your organization with Low Carbon Diet – Are you involved in a local, regional or national group committed to helping people reduce their carbon footprint? If so, Empowerment Institute invites you to sign your group up as a *Low Carbon Diet* Partner. This fundraising opportunity allows you to promote the book through your newsletter, via email, on your website, or with a printed flier—and receive a donation for each book sold. If you're interested in becoming a *Low Carbon Diet* Partner, visit www.empowermentinstitute.net/lcd or email: lcd@empowermentinstitute.net.

Spread the word about Low Carbon Diet *with a printable flier* – Empower your friends, family, co-workers, clients and faith community to reduce their CO_2 footprint. Visit www.empowermentinstitute.net/lcd and print out a stack of flyers on your home or office printer, and pass them around, leave them on information tables at events, etc.

EMPOWERMENT INSTITUTE PROGRAMS

Changing the World: The Craft of Transformative Leadership – This two-day training provides skills and inspiration for leaders implementing transformative change in an organization or community. It is customized for organizations or communities. For more information visit www.empowermentinstitute.net/files/TLT.html.

Livable Neighborhood Program: Making Life Better on the Street Where You Live – This program has been successfully used in many communities to help neighbors improve the quality of life on their block. The action format is similar to the *Low Carbon Diet* but it is done as a team rather than an individual household. The program is divided into four sections: neighborhood health and safety, neighborhood beautification and greening, neighborhood resource sharing, and neighborhood community building. For more information visit www.empowermentinstitute.net.

All Together Now: Neighbors Helping Neighbors Create a Disaster Resilient Community – This program is currently being rolled out in NYC to help residents prepare for natural disasters, terrorist incidents, emergencies or an avian flu pandemic. It uses the same action format as the *Low Carbon Diet* and is done either as a team or single household. It is designed to create disaster resilient blocks and buildings. For more information visit www.empowermentinstitute.net/atn.

EcoTeam: Empowering Americans to Create Earth Friendly Lifestyles – This is the mother program that has been adapted for 22 countries. It is designed to help participants create environmentally sustainable lifestyles. It focuses on garbage, water, energy, transportation, and purchasing. It can be done as a single household or EcoTeam. For more information visit www.empowermentinstitute.net/files/SLP.html.

Journey for the Planet: A Kids' Five Week Adventure to Create an Earth Friendly Lifestyle – This is the children's version of the EcoTeam program. It can be done by children on their own or as part of a classroom or youth group. A teacher's curriculum is available for use in the classroom. This program is described in the "Cool School" action of the *Low Carbon Diet*. For more information visit www.empowermentinstitute.net/files/JFP.html.

Water Stewardship Program – This program is designed to help neighborhoods and communities that are challenged by water quality or water conservation issues. It helps households develop practices to reduce their impact on local water bodies and conserve water in droughts. It can be done either as an individual household or a team. For more information visit www.empowermentinstitute.net.

Dream for Our World: This book tells the mythic story of the First Earth Run and provides 7 practices that grew out of it for changing the world. For more information visit www.empowermentinstitute.net/dream.

BOOK ORDERS

To order copies of this book (quantity discount available) go to: www.empowermentinstitute.net/lcd and click on "Purchase the Book."